MW01001049

This book belongs to

Alice

Given by

Grandpa Eric, Vergy

Date

11/25/15

Sacred Heart of Jesus, have mercy on us.

A Note to Parents

This volume is designed to help your child see the value and joy of praying. As St. Paul said, "Rejoice always. Pray constantly" (1 Thess. 5: 16-17).

Your child should learn from the earliest ages that praying is to be done everywhere and at all times, not just in Church. Our Catholic faith is rich with devotional traditions and practices that serve as little acts of prayer. We should cross ourselves when an ambulance passes by or when we drive past a Catholic Church. We give thanks to God before each meal and ask for His mercy before we go to bed. We pray for our enemies as soon as they offend us. Imagine if all children practiced their faith in this way!

We at Saint Benedict Press hope this little prayer book inspires your child to speak to God throughout the day. May God bless you as you raise your child in the Catholic faith.

Dedication

This book is dedicated to our Blessed Mother and St. Joseph.

Scripture quotations are from the Revised Standard Version of the Bible—Second Catholic Edition (Ignatius Edition). Copyright ©2006 Division of Christian Education of the National Council of the Churches of Christ in the United States of America. Used by permission. All rights reserved.

Compiled by Conor Gallagher.

Illustration and design by Chris Pelicano.

Published in the United States by Saint Benedict Press, LLC.
PO Box 410487
Charlotte, NC 28241
www.saintbenedictpress.com
www.tanbooks.com
1-800-437-5876

Pray Always

A Catholic Child's
First Prayer Book

Saint Benedict Press

*"Know that the Lord is God!
It is He that made us, and we are His;
we are His people, and the sheep of His pasture."*

Psalm 100:3

TABLE OF CONTENTS

Dear Boys and Girls   6

Daily Prayers   8

Prayer to My Guardian Angel   14

Prayer to St. Michael the Archangel   15

Prayer Before and After Meals   16

Praying the Holy Rosary   17

Mysteries of the Holy Rosary   18

Prayer to Mary for My Mother   20

Prayer to St. Joseph for My Father   21

Examination of Conscience   22

Act of Contrition   23

Prayer Before and After Holy Communion   24

Good Times to Pray   26

Praying with the Saints   28

The Little Way of St. Thérèse   29

A Boy's Prayer to St. Martin de Porres   30

A Girl's Prayer to St. Rose of Lima   32

St. Francis of Assisi   34

St. Bernadette   35

St. Jude   36

St. Joan of Arc   37

Bl. Pier Giorgio Frassati   38

St. (Padre) Pio   39

St. Faustina Kowalska   40

St. John the Apostle   41

St. Elizabeth Ann Seton   42

St. John Paul II   43

Litany of the Sacred Heart of Jesus   44

Litany of the Blessed Virgin Mary   46

The Divine Praises   48

Dear Boys and Girls,

This is your own prayer book. Take it with you to Mass. Use it to help you say your prayers at bedtime and in the morning. Read it a little bit every day.

Every page has a prayer and a picture. Some pictures are of angels or saints. Remember that they are your friends in heaven. Ask them to protect you.

Some of the pictures in this prayer book are of Jesus' mother, Mary. She is also your mother, and you are her child. Speak to her. Ask her for help. Tell her why you are happy or sad. She will always listen to you.

Some of the pictures in this book are of Jesus, your Savior. He is God, but He is also a human being. He was a child, just like you! He gives us Himself in the Eucharist. And He will one day welcome you into heaven.

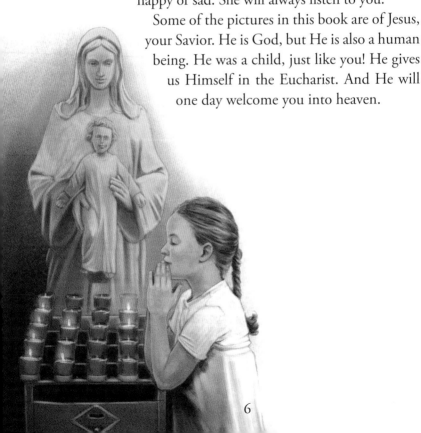

Finally, you will see pictures of children saying their prayers before bedtime, while doing schoolwork, while playing games, and at other times, too. These pictures should remind you that you can pray at almost any time during the day. Jesus and the saints want you to pray always and often during your daily activities.

Praying often will help you to become a saint and get to heaven to be with Jesus and Mary forever.

We love you and we will pray for you, too.

The Publishers

"Lord, I am continually with You;
You hold my right hand."

Psalm 73:23

DAILY PRAYERS

Morning Prayer

O my God, I offer you every thought and word and act of this day. Please bless me, my God, and make me good today. Amen.

Evening Prayer

O God, thank You for the many blessings of this day. Thank you for my family and friends and all the people I love. Please take care of the sick and the poor and all who need a special blessing from You tonight.

I am sorry for my sins today. Please forgive me. Bless me while I sleep and help me be holy tomorrow. Amen.

DAILY PRAYERS

The Sign of the Cross

In the name of the Father, and of the Son, and of the Holy Spirit. Amen.

The Our Father

Our Father, who art in heaven, hallowed be Thy name. Thy kingdom come. Thy will be done, on earth as it is in heaven. Give us this day our daily bread, and forgive us our trespasses, as we forgive those who trespass against us. And lead us not into temptation, but deliver us from evil. Amen.

The Hail Mary

Hail Mary, full of grace, the Lord is with thee. Blessed art thou among women, and blessed is the fruit of thy womb, Jesus. Holy Mary, Mother of God, pray for us sinners now and at the hour of our death. Amen.

The Glory Be

Glory be to the Father, and to the Son, and to the Holy Spirit. As it was in the beginning, is now, and ever shall be, world without end. Amen.

DAILY PRAYERS

The Apostles' Creed

I believe in God, the Father Almighty, creator of heaven and earth; and in Jesus Christ, His only Son, Our Lord, who was conceived by the Holy Spirit, born of the Virgin Mary, suffered under Pontius Pilate, was crucified, died, and was buried. He descended into hell; the third day He rose again from the dead; He ascended into heaven, and is seated at the right hand of God, the Father almighty; from thence He shall come to judge the living and the dead. I believe in the Holy Spirit, the holy Catholic Church, the communion of saints, the forgiveness of sins, the resurrection of the body, and the life everlasting. Amen.

*Sweet Heart of Jesus,
be my love!*

DAILY PRAYERS

Act of Faith

O my God, I believe in You, and I believe all that the Holy Catholic Church teaches.

Act of Hope

O my God, I hope in You; please forgive my sins and lead me to heaven.

Act of Love

O my God, I love You with all my heart and soul because You are so great and so good.

DAILY PRAYERS

A Prayer to the Holy Spirit

O Holy Spirit, beloved of my soul, I adore You. Enlighten me, guide me, strengthen me, console me. Tell me what I should do; give me Your orders. I promise to submit myself to all that You desire of me and to accept all that You permit to happen to me. Let me only know Your will. Amen.

Hail, Holy Queen

Hail, holy Queen, mother of mercy, our life, our sweetness and our hope! To thee do we cry, poor banished children of Eve; to thee do we send up our sighs, mourning and weeping in this valley of tears. Turn then, most gracious advocate, thine eyes of mercy toward us, and after this our exile, show unto us the blessed fruit of thy womb, Jesus. O clement, O loving, O sweet Virgin Mary!

Pray for us, O holy Mother of God.
That we may be made worthy of the promises of Christ.
Amen.

DAILY PRAYERS

Prayer for My Family

Heavenly Father, I thank You for my family and for our home. Please bless *(name your family members)*.

Help us all to love You and to serve one another as Jesus taught us to do. Give me strength to do what is right today and to do for others what I would want them to do for me. Amen.

PRAYER TO MY GUARDIAN ANGEL

Angel of God, my guardian dear,
to whom God's love commits me here,
ever this day be at my side,
to light and guard, to rule and guide.
Amen.

PRAYER TO ST. MICHAEL THE ARCHANGEL

St. Michael the Archangel, defend us in battle. Be our protection against the wickedness and snares of the Devil. May God rebuke him, we humbly pray, and do thou, O prince of the heavenly hosts, by the power of God, thrust into hell Satan and all the evil spirits, who prowl about the world seeking the ruin of souls. Amen.

PRAYERS AT MEALS

Prayer Before Meals

Bless us, O Lord, and these Your gifts, which we are about to receive from Your bounty, through Christ our Lord. Amen.

Prayer After Meals

We thank You, O God, for these gifts and for all the gifts we have received from Your goodness, through Christ our Lord. Amen.

PRAYING THE HOLY ROSARY

How to Pray the Holy Rosary of the Blessed Virgin Mary

Follow the numbers from 1 to 15.

1. **To begin,** make the Sign of the Cross and pray the Apostles' Creed.
2. Pray the Our Father.
3. Pray three Hail Marys.
4. Pray the Glory Be.
5. Announce the First Mystery and pray the Our Father.
6. **THE FIRST MYSTERY:** Pray 10 Hail Marys and a Glory Be.
7. Announce the Second Mystery and pray the Our Father.
8. **THE SECOND MYSTERY:** Pray 10 Hail Marys and a Glory Be.
9. Announce the Third Mystery and pray the Our Father.
10. **THE THIRD MYSTERY:** Pray 10 Hail Marys and a Glory Be.

Families that pray together, stay together.

11. Announce the Fourth Mystery and pray the Our Father.
12. **THE FOURTH MYSTERY:** Pray 10 Hail Marys and a Glory Be.
13. Announce the Fifth Mystery and pray the Our Father.
14. **THE FIFTH MYSTERY:** Pray 10 Hail Marys and a Glory Be.
15. **To finish,** pray the Hail, Holy Queen; end on the crucifix with the Sign of the Cross.

17

MYSTERIES OF THE HOLY ROSARY
The Joyful Mysteries
Prayed on Monday and Saturday

1. **The Annunciation:** The angel Gabriel announces to Mary that she will have a baby, and Mary says yes to God. How can we say yes to God, too?
2. **The Visitation:** Mary goes to help her cousin Elizabeth, who would soon have a baby as well. How can we, too, help our families?
3. **The Nativity:** Nativity means "birth." How should we celebrate the birth of Jesus?
4. **The Presentation:** Mary and Joseph go to the Temple to present the great gift of the Child that God has given them. How can we, too, present Jesus to others?
5. **The Finding of Jesus in the Temple:** After the festival in Jerusalem, Mary and Joseph cannot find Jesus. They finally discover Him in the Temple talking to the teachers there. How can we learn from our teachers?

The Luminous Mysteries
Prayed on Thursday

1. **The Baptism of Jesus:** As Jesus is baptized in the Jordan River, the Holy Spirit comes on Him, and God the Father speaks. How does God speak to us?
2. **The Miracle at the Wedding Feast of Cana:** Jesus' mother tells Him that the wedding guests have run out of wine. So Jesus turns jars of water into wine for them, His first miracle. Do we, too, ask Jesus to help us with whatever we need?
3. **The Proclamation of the Kingdom and the Call to Conversion:** When Jesus says, "The kingdom of God is at hand" (Mark 1:15), that means it's time for God's work to be seen in Jesus' life and death. How does God work through us, too?
4. **The Transfiguration:** Jesus' face shines as bright as the sun as He stands on the mountaintop with Moses and Elijah. God's voice tells the disciples to listen to His Son. How can we let Jesus shine in us?
5. **The First Eucharist:** Jesus blesses bread and wine, then tells His disciples that the bread has now become His Body, and the wine is now His Blood. This is the first Holy Communion. How can we get ourselves ready to receive Jesus' Body and Blood in Communion?

MYSTERIES OF THE HOLY ROSARY
The Sorrowful Mysteries
Prayed on Tuesday and Friday

1. **The Agony in the Garden:** In a garden called Gethsemane, Jesus feels the sadness of His coming death. But the sadness can't keep Him from doing what God wants. Do we obey God, too, even when it's hard?
2. **The Scourging at the Pillar:** Soldiers tie Jesus to a pillar and beat Him. Jesus suffers for all of us. How do we help others who are suffering?
3. **The Crowning with Thorns:** Soldiers take off Jesus' clothes and place a crown of thorns on His head. They make fun of Him and speak to Him cruelly. Do we comfort Jesus instead by telling Him how much we love Him?
4. **The Carrying of the Cross:** Jesus carries the cross that will be used to crucify Him. When we're hurting, do we offer our suffering to Jesus to help Him carry His cross?
5. **The Crucifixion:** The soldiers hang Jesus on the cross to die. Jesus hangs there for each one of us, because He loves us so much! Do we thank Jesus often for giving His life for us?

The Glorious Mysteries
Prayed on Wednesday and Sunday

1. **The Resurrection:** By rising from the dead, Jesus gives us life forever. We were given that new life when we were baptized. Do we try to live the same way Jesus lived, with kindness toward everyone?
2. **The Ascension:** Jesus is taken up to heaven, where He wants us to come and live with Him forever. When we become discouraged, do we think about heaven, and thank God for His plans for us?
3. **The Descent of the Holy Spirit:** The Holy Spirit comes upon the disciples, and they speak the languages of all the different people around. They tell them about God, and many people are baptized. How does the Holy Spirit come to us?
4. **The Assumption:** Mary, the Mother of God and our mother, is taken up to heaven, where she prays for us. Do we ask Mary to help us become more like her Son, Jesus?
5. **The Coronation:** The mother of a King is the Queen Mother. Jesus is the King of heaven, so His mother, Mary, was crowned the Queen of Heaven alongside Him. In what ways can we honor Mary, our mother and our queen?

PRAYER TO MARY FOR MY MOTHER

Dear Blessed Mother Mary, please help my mother be a good mother. Give her joy when she is sad and rest when she is tired. Ask your Son, Jesus, to forgive her when she sins.

Help me show my mother how much I love her, just as Jesus showed you how much He loved you. Amen.

Pray for us, O Holy Mother of God,
that we may be made worthy of the promises of Christ.

PRAYER TO ST. JOSEPH FOR MY FATHER

Dear St. Joseph, please help my father be a good father. Give him strength when he is weak and wisdom when he is confused. Ask your foster Son, Jesus, to forgive him when he sins.

Help me show my father how much I love him, just as Jesus showed you how much He loved you. Amen.

Jesus, Mary, and Joseph!

EXAMINATION OF CONSCIENCE

When I obey God's commandments I am showing Him my love. I will try to find out my sins by asking myself these questions. This will help to make me ready when I go to Confession.

- Have I forgotten to say my prayers each day?
- Have I used holy names such as "God" and "Jesus" in an unholy way?
- Have I complained about going to Mass on Sundays?
- Have I disobeyed or been disrespectful to my mother and father or those who take the place of my parents?
- Have I been angry or fought with my family or friends?
- Have I told a lie?
- Have I stolen anything?
- Have I told mean things about other people?

When you go to confession, be sure to tell the priest how many times you have committed a sin.

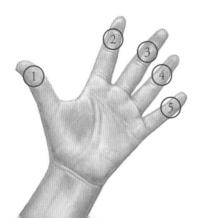

The five things you need to do to make a good confession:

1. Know your sins.

2. Be sorry for your sins.

3. Decide to avoid sinning again.

4. Confess your sins to the priest.

5. Do the penance the priest gives you.

ACT OF CONTRITION

O my God, I am heartily sorry for having offended You, and I detest all my sins because of Your just punishment, but most of all because they offend You, my God, who are all-good and deserving of all my love.

I firmly resolve, with the help of Your grace, to sin no more and to avoid the near occasion of sin. Amen.

PRAYER BEFORE
HOLY COMMUNION

Sweet Jesus, with this Holy Communion, I offer You today my thoughts, my words, and all that I do. Let Your grace help me to be always ready to receive You. Amen.

My Lord and my God!

My God and my All!

PRAYER AFTER
HOLY COMMUNION

Sweet Jesus, Your miracles are very great. Your greatest miracle is to give Your Body and Blood to us in Holy Communion. I know that this is You Yourself, and not just bread.

I thank You for giving Yourself to me. Let this Holy Communion bring me closer to You, my Lord and my God. Amen.

I AM THE BREAD OF LIFE

Blessed be God in the Most Holy Sacrament of the Altar!

Good Times to Pray
THE SIGN OF THE CROSS

Pray the Sign of the Cross reverently when you use holy water when entering or leaving a Catholic church or home.

Pray the Sign of the Cross reverently when you pass in front of Jesus in the tabernacle when you are inside a Catholic church and even when you are driving by one.

Pray the Sign of the Cross reverently when you genuflect in front of Jesus in the tabernacle when you enter and leave your pew in church.

Good Times to Pray
SHORT PRAYERS

Pray a short prayer that God will help people in danger whenever you see or hear an emergency vehicle such as an ambulance, fire truck, or police car.

Pray a short prayer that God will help you and your classmates to concentrate on school work. Give thanks to God when you are finished working.

Pray a short prayer that God will help you and your friends to play fairly, do your best, and not get hurt. Pray for the players on the other team as well.

PRAYING WITH THE SAINTS

Why We Honor the Saints and Pray to Them

When we love God, we love others, too. We want to help them. So we pray to God for them, and we try to set a good example to show them how to love God as well.

God has given us a loving spiritual family in heaven. We call them the saints, and they want to help us.

When they lived on this earth, they set a good example for loving God and others. So we want to be like them.

Now that these saints are in heaven, they love us even more. They are closer than ever to God, so they know His mind and His heart even better than they did on earth. They can pray for us in a perfect way, asking Him to do for us what is best.

When we honor the saints, we thank them for their help, and we seek to follow their example. When we pray to the saints, we ask them to pray with us that God will make us holy. That way, after we have lived a life of love on this earth, we can go home to heaven. Then we, too, will be saints who live with God forever.

The Little Way of St. Thérèse

St. Thérèse of Lisieux (1873–1897) was the youngest of nine children. Her mother died when Thérèse was only four years old. Sometimes she was selfish and very sad because she missed her mother. But her father and her older siblings loved her very much and helped Thérèse to be good. Do you love your family?

When Thérèse was fourteen years old, she decided to stop complaining about her chores and about other people. She lovingly gave her whole heart to Jesus. Did you know that you can also give your heart to Jesus and become a saint?

Thérèse said that little acts of kindness and forgiveness make Jesus very happy. She called this her "little way" of love. She wants you to respect your parents, be kind to your siblings, and say your prayers every day. This can be your "little way" of love, and you can become holy, too, just like St. Thérèse.

A BOY'S PRAYER
TO ST. MARTIN DE PORRES

Dear St. Martin de Porres, you were a great example of how to be holy as a boy and a young man. You were humble and kind. You prayed every day, you worked hard at your chores, and you cared for all who needed your help—even the animals. I want to be holy like you!

Show me how to be strong, generous, and patient. Help me to love Jesus and all those around me, so that one day I may join you and many other holy boys in heaven. There we can all worship God together! Amen.

Who was St. Martin de Porres?

St. Martin de Porres (1579–1639) lived in Lima, Peru. His mother was quite poor and had once been a slave, so people looked down on Martin. But he grew up with a great faith in God that made him patient and humble, even though he was often mistreated.

Spending time talking to God every day made Martin very happy. Because of his love for Jesus, he often shared what little food he had with those who were homeless. He cared for the sick as well, and he had a special gift for helping animals, such as dogs and cats and even mice!

Martin wanted to give his life to God. So when he was only fifteen, he went to live in a house of men who were followers of St. Dominic. He became their young helper, and every day he worked hard doing chores around the house, such as cooking, cleaning, and washing clothes.

As he grew into a young man, Martin became known all over the city of Lima for his kindness in caring for others and for working miracles to help them. To this day, Martin is still remembered as the friend of all those in need.

A GIRL'S PRAYER
TO ST. ROSE OF LIMA

Dear St. Rose of Lima, you show me how to be holy as a girl and a young woman. You gave your life to Jesus. You prayed daily and made sacrifices for God, and you worked hard to care for your family, the sick, and the poor. I want to be holy like you!

Teach me how to have faith in God and to serve others. Help me to love Jesus and all those around me, so that one day I may join you in heaven with many other girls who love Him. There we can all worship God together! Amen.

Who was St. Rose of Lima?

Saint Rose of Lima (1586–1617) was born in Lima, Peru, and was a friend of St. Martin de Porres. While still very young, she gave her life to Jesus. As a child, she spent most of her time in prayer and hard work. But she also played, with birds and even mosquitoes as her playmates!

Rose cared for the family garden. She raised vegetables for the family to eat, flowers to sell in the market, and herbs for medicine to help sick people. She also created beautiful lace and embroidery, selling it to raise money for her family and for the poor.

At the age of nineteen, Rose became a follower of St. Dominic. But instead of living as a nun in a convent, she remained at home. She continued to spend many hours in prayer and making sacrifices for God. She also continued to care for the sick and the poor.

Although Rose loved God with all her heart, she still struggled with temptations. Sometimes she felt sad or lonely. But she cheerfully offered up to God all her troubles. We can learn from her example to love God and to trust Him in all things.

ST. FRANCIS OF ASSISI
(1181–1226)

St. Francis of Assisi was a little man with a big love for God's creatures. The plants, the animals, the sun, and the moon made him very joyful. He shared this joy with the poor and lonely.

Prayer to help me take care of my pets

St. Francis, sometimes I forget that my pet is not a toy, but a gift from God to be my friend. You loved all of God's creatures because God loves them. Help me to take good care of my pet and to thank God for His gift to me. Amen.

ST. BERNADETTE
(1844–1879)

St. Bernadette was a little girl when Mary appeared to her in Lourdes, France. Thousands of sick people have been cured by miracles at the place where Mary appeared to her. Bernadette was often sick, but she still worked hard to care for other sick people.

Prayer to take care of sick people

St. Bernadette, I know someone who is sick. It makes me sad. You cared for sick people with gentleness and love. Please ask Mary to help this person. Help me to be gentle and loving, even when I don't feel like it. Amen.

ST. JUDE
(first century)

St. Jude was one of the twelve apostles. He was a friend of Jesus. Lots of people were scared when Jesus died. Jude encouraged people to pray to God when they were in trouble and afraid. Jude spends his time in heaven helping children when they are in trouble.

Prayer when I'm scared

St. Jude, I'm a little scared about something right now. I don't know what will happen. You helped the early Christians who were afraid, and now you help lots of children who are afraid. Help me have faith in God and hope in His mercy so that I won't be so afraid. Amen.

ST. JOAN OF ARC
(1412–1431)

St. Joan of Arc was a young girl who was more brave than all the grownup men in the army. She became a warrior in the army and won many battles. Like little David who fought Goliath, Joan had faith that God would protect her. Joan loves little children and helps them to be brave when they must face difficulty.

Prayer for courage

St. Joan of Arc, I don't always want to be brave. Sometimes I want to hide from difficult things in life. You were brave because you had lots of faith in God. Please help me be brave so that I can do everything God wants me to do. Amen.

BL. PIER GIORGIO FRASSATI
(1901–1925)

Blessed Pier Giorgio was a young boy who loved sports and having fun with his friends. He used sports to help teach his friends about God. Now that he is in heaven, Pier Giorgio helps children be kind, even while competing with others.

Prayer to be a good sport

Bl. Pier Giorgio, I hate losing games. Sometimes I can get jealous and angry when I lose, especially when the winner rubs it in. You were always a good sport, even if you lost a game. Help me be kind to the other team, even if they win. I know that God cares more about my soul than how many trophies I win. Amen.

ST. (PADRE) PIO
(1887–1968)

Padre Pio was a priest who had many spiritual gifts. He had the wounds of Christ on his hands and feet. He had the gift of healing sick people. God often told him what was in the hearts of other people. He used this gift to help others make good confessions.

Prayer for a good confession

St. Pio, I know that going to confession is good, but sometimes I forget what to say. Sometimes I'm embarrassed to tell the priest all of my sins. You helped people make good confessions during your life. Now that you're in heaven, please help me to be honest and make a good confession. Amen.

ST. FAUSTINA KOWALSKA
(1905–1938)

St. Faustina Kowalska was a nun. Jesus appeared to her to show His merciful heart as a sign of His love for sinners. St. Faustina spent the rest of her life teaching and writing about Jesus' mercy for the whole world.

Prayer to forgive others

St. Faustina, it's hard to forgive people who are mean to me. Jesus loves to forgive a sinner. He also loves to see me forgive a sinner. Help me to forgive other people as Jesus forgives me. Amen.

ST. JOHN THE APOSTLE
(first century)

St. John was the youngest apostle of Jesus. He was good friends with Jesus. John fished with Him, ate with Him, and laughed with Him. John was such good friends with Jesus that he stood by the cross when Jesus died. After Jesus died, John also took care of Jesus' mother, Mary.

Prayer for good friendships

St. John, some of the people I play with are not good examples for me. I know lots of people my age, but I need more good friendships. You were friends with Jesus and His mother, Mary. Please help surround me with good boys and girls who will help me to be holy. Please keep me safe from bullies and bad children who will lead me away from God. Amen.

ST. ELIZABETH ANN SETON
(1774–1821)

St. Elizabeth Ann Seton was a wife, mother, and teacher. When her husband died, she made money teaching young children how to read and write. When her own children grew up, she became a religious sister and spent the rest of her life helping children.

Prayer to be a good student

St. Elizabeth Ann Seton, I get tired of doing my schoolwork. I'd rather play with my friends. You understand my feelings because you worked with children for many years while you were on earth. Now that you're in heaven, please help me do my schoolwork with a happy heart. Amen.

ST. JOHN PAUL II
(1920–2005)

St. John Paul II loved skiing, hiking, and playing soccer. He loved the outdoors because it reminded him of God's power and love. After he became the Pope, he still made sure to go skiing and hiking. He thanked God for His beautiful creation.

Prayer for outdoor activities

St. John Paul II, I love playing outside. When you were a child, you played with great joy because of your love for God. Please keep me safe, and help me have fun and remember that God is the creator of all the wonderful things outside. Amen.

LITANY OF THE
SACRED HEART OF JESUS

Lord, have mercy on us.
Christ, have mercy on us.
Lord, have mercy on us. Christ, hear us.
Christ, graciously hear us.

God the Father of Heaven, *have mercy on us.*
God the Son, Redeemer of the world, *have mercy on us.*
God the Holy Spirit, *have mercy on us.*
Holy Trinity, one God, *have mercy on us.*

Heart of Jesus, Son of the Eternal Father, *have mercy on us.*
Heart of Jesus, formed by the Holy Spirit in the womb of the
Virgin Mother. *(Repeat "have mercy on us" after each.)*
Heart of Jesus, one with the eternal Word.
Heart of Jesus, of infinite majesty.
Heart of Jesus, holy temple of God.
Heart of Jesus, tabernacle of the Most High.
Heart of Jesus, house of God and gate of heaven.
Heart of Jesus, aflame with love for us.
Heart of Jesus, source of justice and love.
Heart of Jesus, full of goodness and love.
Heart of Jesus, wellspring of all virtue.
Heart of Jesus, worthy of all praise.
Heart of Jesus, King and center of all hearts.
Heart of Jesus, treasure-house of wisdom and knowledge.
Heart of Jesus, in whom there dwells the fullness of God.
Heart of Jesus, in whom the Father is well pleased.
Heart of Jesus, from whose fullness we have all received.

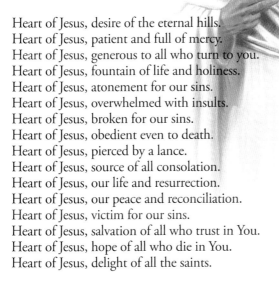

Heart of Jesus, desire of the eternal hills.
Heart of Jesus, patient and full of mercy.
Heart of Jesus, generous to all who turn to you.
Heart of Jesus, fountain of life and holiness.
Heart of Jesus, atonement for our sins.
Heart of Jesus, overwhelmed with insults.
Heart of Jesus, broken for our sins.
Heart of Jesus, obedient even to death.
Heart of Jesus, pierced by a lance.
Heart of Jesus, source of all consolation.
Heart of Jesus, our life and resurrection.
Heart of Jesus, our peace and reconciliation.
Heart of Jesus, victim for our sins.
Heart of Jesus, salvation of all who trust in You.
Heart of Jesus, hope of all who die in You.
Heart of Jesus, delight of all the saints.

Lamb of God, you take away the sins of the world, *spare us, O Lord.*
Lamb of God, you take away the sins of the world, *graciously hear us.*
Lamb of God, you take away the sins of the world, *have mercy on us.*

Jesus, gentle and humble of heart,
Touch our hearts and make them like your own.

Father, we rejoice in the gifts of love we have received from the heart of Jesus your Son. Open our hearts to share his life and continue to bless us with his love. We ask this in the name of Jesus the Lord. Amen.

LITANY OF THE BLESSED VIRGIN MARY

Lord, have mercy on us. *Christ, have mercy on us.*
Lord, have mercy on us. Christ, hear us. *Christ, graciously hear us.*
God the Father of Heaven, *have mercy on us.*
God the Son, Redeemer of the world, *have mercy on us.*
God the Holy Spirit, *have mercy on us.*
Holy Trinity, one God, *have mercy on us.*

Holy Mary, *pray for us.*
Holy Mother of God, *pray for us.*
Most honored of virgins, *pray for us.*
Mother of Christ, *pray for us.*
Mother of the Church, *pray for us.*
Mother of divine grace, *pray for us.*
Mother most pure, *pray for us.*
Mother of chaste love, *pray for us.*
Mother and virgin, *pray for us.*
Sinless mother, *pray for us.*
Dearest of mothers, *pray for us.*
Model of motherhood, *pray for us.*
Mother of good counsel, *pray for us.*
Mother of our Creator, *pray for us.*
Mother of our Savior, *pray for us.*
Virgin most wise, *pray for us.*
Virgin rightly praised, *pray for us.*
Virgin rightly renowned, *pray for us.*
Virgin most powerful, *pray for us.*
Virgin gentle in mercy, *pray for us.*
Faithful virgin, *pray for us.*
Mirror of justice, *pray for us.*
Throne of wisdom, *pray for us.*
Cause of our joy, *pray for us.*
Shrine of the Spirit, *pray for us.*
Glory of Israel, *pray for us.*
Vessel of selfless devotion, *pray for us.*

Mystical rose, *pray for us.*
Tower of David, *pray for us.*
Tower of ivory, *pray for us.*
House of gold, *pray for us.*
Ark of the Covenant, *pray for us.*
Gate of heaven, *pray for us.*
Morning star, *pray for us.*
Health of the sick, *pray for us.*
Refuge of sinners, *pray for us.*
Comfort of the troubled, *pray for us.*
Help of Christians, *pray for us.*
Queen of angels, *pray for us.*
Queen of patriarchs and prophets, *pray for us.*
Queen of apostles and martyrs, *pray for us.*
Queen of confessors and virgins, *pray for us.*
Queen of all saints, *pray for us.*
Queen conceived without original sin, *pray for us.*
Queen assumed into heaven, *pray for us.*
Queen of the Rosary, *pray for us.*
Queen of families, *pray for us.*
Queen of peace, *pray for us.*

Lamb of God, you take away the sins of the world, s*pare us, O Lord.*
Lamb of God, you take away the sins of the world, *graciously hear us.*
Lamb of God, you take away the sins of the world, *have mercy on us.*

Pray for us, holy Mother of God, *that we may be made worthy of the promises of Christ.*

Grant, we beseech you, O Lord God, that we, your servants, may enjoy perpetual health of mind and body; and by the intercession of Blessed Mary, ever Virgin, may be delivered from present sorrow, and obtain eternal joy. Through Christ our Lord. Amen.

THE DIVINE PRAISES

Blessed be God.
Blessed be His Holy Name.
Blessed be Jesus Christ, true God and true Man.
Blessed be the name of Jesus.
Blessed be His Most Sacred Heart.
Blessed be His Most Precious Blood.
Blessed be Jesus in the Most Holy Sacrament of the Altar.
Blessed be the Holy Spirit, the paraclete.
Blessed be the great Mother of God, Mary most holy.
Blessed be her holy and Immaculate Conception.
Blessed be her glorious Assumption.
Blessed be the name of Mary, Virgin and Mother.
Blessed be St. Joseph, her most chaste spouse.
Blessed be God in His angels and in His saints.